S0-BLA-154

# INVENTIONS
## *That Made History*

Here are thirty-two inventions that dramatically affected man and his civilization. From the printing press to the laser beam, to date the most amazing device ever conceived, man demonstrates an amazing capacity to find new ways to improve his existence. Each invention is chronicled and illustrated. The author reveals that most of man's important inventions were the result of long years of painstaking work, often spanning more than a century, as one generation of scientists and technicians picked up the reins from their predecessors.

# INVENTIONS

## *That Made History*

BY
DAVID C. COOKE

G. P. PUTNAM'S SONS NEW YORK

*To the entire Thiem family—*
*Albert, Caroline, Susan, and Albee*



Library of Congress Catalog Card Number: 68-24508
PRINTED IN THE UNITED STATES OF AMERICA.

10 up

# Contents

Books by David C. Cooke in this series

Fighter Planes That Made History
Bomber Planes That Made History
Transport Planes That Made History
Racing Cars That Made History
Racing Planes That Made History
Flights That Made History
Jet and Rocket Planes That Made History
Dirigibles That Made History
Seaplanes That Made History
Helicopters That Made History
Inventions That Made History

# FOREWORD

Of all the abilities possessed by mankind, perhaps the most important is that of imagination. This one ability makes people different from all the other creatures in the animal kingdom.

Since men first walked the earth they have been forced to put their imagination to work. It was too difficult to drag heavy objects, and so they invented the wheel. They were weaker than many other animals, and so they invented the spear and the bow and arrow. They could not swim as well as fish, and so they made rafts to cross rivers or float downstream. They could not run rapidly or carry heavy loads, so they tamed horses and other animals to work for them.

Imagination has been the motivating force behind every invention from toothpicks to television, from matches to motion pictures, from nails to nylon, from anchors to atomic energy.

According to the dictionary, the word "invent" means to "create or devise in the imagination." Very simply, this means to think of something that is needed, or to think of a better way to do something.

Almost everybody invents something at one time or another. Some of these inventions might help other people, and some help only ourselves. However, they are all products of imagination, of the constant striving to do something or make something better.

Men of imagination have contributed to society through the ages. Buttons, zippers, fountain pens, safety pins, paper cups – these are all inventions to make something better or to do a certain job.

Some of the inventions that men of imagination have created have gone down in the history books as being among the greatest contributions to society. Of all the millions of things that have been created by men, I have attempted to assemble the most notable for inclusion in this book. I have also attempted to give the true story of each of these, and have presented them in their approximate order of appearance.

It would not be possible to list the names of all the people and organizations which helped me in my quest for information, but some of these are given in the credit lines accompanying the photographs. I would also like to thank all the others who helped but are not mentioned by name. – DAVID C. COOKE

## PRINTING

Around the year 1455 the learned men of Europe were startled to see something new: a Bible in Latin, printed in 1,282 pages. This was not the first Bible, nor was it the first in Latin. However, it was the first book they had seen that was printed from type rather than written slowly by hand.

The Gutenberg Bible, as it became known, was not actually the first book that Johann Gutenberg of Mainz, Germany, had printed with his movable type. About five years previously he had produced a much smaller book, but the Bible was his finest work and was destined to make a place for him in history.

Europeans thought that Gutenberg was the first person to use movable type, but this was not so. Printing had been developed in the Orient around A.D. 400, and between 1041 and 1049 a Chinese named Pi Sheng made the first movable type of earthenware. Movable metal type was first made in Korea in 1241, but the name of the inventor is not known.

Before the invention of movable type, printing was done from wooden blocks into which each letter and word was carved by hand. With movable type, the same type could be used many times, thus making the process much faster.

But even after printers had movable type, their presses were still extremely slow. All printing presses were made of wood, and paper was pressed against the inked type by turning down a screw. Then, in 1772, Wilhelm Haas of Switzerland made the first cast-iron press. By 1800, these presses could produce up to 300 sheets per hour—as many as Gutenberg had been able to print in an entire day.

The first steam-powered printing press was made in 1814 by Friedrich Koening, a German. His press printed a thousand sheets per hour. Then in 1845 an American, Richard Hoe, invented a press that printed on a continuous roll of paper. This was called a rotary press.

With the development of modern printing presses, the age of books, magazines, and newspapers for all had arrived.



**The first Hoe rotary press printed on sheets of paper rather than a roll.**
***(The Smithsonian Institution)***

# STEAM ENGINE

The world's first known steam engine was invented by Hero in ancient Greece around the year 120 B.C. Hero called his device an *aeolipile*, naming it after Aeolus, the god of the winds. While the aeolipile was in essence a steam turbine, it was never considered anything more than a strange but wonderful toy.

Several men following Hero tried to use the power of steam to perform various types of work. Some of these machines were weird; one of them, a metal figure of a man, blew steam to turn a paddle wheel, which made weights go up and down to pound various powders into medicines. Steam power continued to be a strange toy with no practical use.

Then, around 1690, Dionysius Papin of France invented the first steam engine with a cylinder and piston. When Papin forced steam into the bottom of his cylinder, the piston was pushed upward by the pressure. After the steam cooled in the cylinder, the piston came down again. Papin had the right idea, but he didn't know what to do with it.

Thomas Newcomen, an English blacksmith, is credited with putting steam to work for the first time. Using the cylinder and piston idea conceived by Papin, he made an engine which would pump water from great depths. This machine saved the coal industry in England. However, Newcomen did not know how to cool the steam in his engine quickly enough, and it could make only twelve or fifteen strokes per minute.

Then one day James Watt, a Scots machinist, was called in to repair a Newcomen engine. Watt recognized the problem of the engine and set about to improve it. He experimented for several years, then finally hit upon an idea: if steam could be used to force the piston up, why not force it down again with more steam from the other side, expelling the used steam through an automatic valve?

Watt had his first engine ready in 1765, and it worked exactly as he had expected. This was the beginning of a new era, for man finally had mechanical power to turn the wheels of industry.



**An early model of Watt's engine, with separate condenser and air pump.**
***(The Smithsonian Institution)***

# POWER LOOM

As recently as only 200 years ago life was difficult in even the most advanced countries. There were no factories as we know them today, and everything had to be made slowly by hand.

Clothing was also difficult to obtain in those days, for all thread had to be spun by hand and all cloth woven by hand-operated machines. This was a very slow and tedious process.

Then, around 1732, a poor English weaver named John Kay got an idea for a method to throw the shuttle back and forth in his loom by pulling on a cord. He called his device the "fly shuttle," and with it he was able to weave much more cloth in a day than ever before.

However, this invention was not enough, for the process of spinning thread was still painfully slow. The first man to come up with a better system was James Hargreaves, who in 1767 made a machine which, by turning a crank, would spin up to eight strands of thread at the same time. He called his device the "spinning jenny," naming it after his wife.

Two years later another Englishman, Richard Arkwright, improved the Hargreaves device and powered it by a water wheel. He called his spinning machine the "water frame." In 1775 Samuel Crompton combined the best features of the spinning jenny and the water frame into his much better "mule," which made the finest thread that anyone had ever seen and also made it much faster.

Suddenly there was a plentiful supply of thread, but weaving was too slow. Then an Englishman named Edmund Cartwright began studying weaving machines, watching the process for hours on end. He came to the conclusion that weaving could be done automatically by machine, and he set about designing one.

Cartwright had his first loom ready in 1787, turning it by a crank. A short time later he added a steam engine for power. This was the true beginning of the Industrial Revolution. Mechanization had begun, and all for the want of material to clothe the people of England.



**Cartwright's loom made low-cost clothing available in large quantities.**
*(The Smithsonian Institution)*

# COTTON GIN

While cotton is one of nature's greatest natural gifts to mankind, it was once considered also something close to a curse because of the long, tedious process of removing seeds from the raw cotton fibers. For centuries this was done by hand, and even the fastest workers could pluck seeds from only a comparatively few pounds of cotton in a working day, which often extended from sunrise to sunset.

In the early history of the United States the country was so underpopulated that cotton farmers could not hire enough people to work their farms effectively. The farmers also wanted to cultivate more land, so they could meet the huge demands of the British textile industry. The only way they could see to get cheap labor, and in sufficient numbers, was to buy African Negroes from the slave traders. However, this was not a new idea, for African slaves had worked cotton fields in other countries for many years before they were brought to the United States.

In 1792 a Massachusetts man named Eli Whitney went to Georgia, where he spent several months on a cotton plantation. This was the first time he had seen the way cotton was grown, picked, and the seeds removed, and he thought it should be possible to develop a machine which could separate the seeds from the cotton without damaging the fibers. The following year he built his first cotton gin, which was to become one of the most important factors in the creation of America's large cotton industry.

Whitney's machine consisted of a cylinder to which a number of sawlike teeth were attached. When the cylinder was revolved, the teeth passed through a fixed comb. As cotton was fed into the machine, the teeth pulled the fibers through and the seeds were left behind. The much larger mechanical cotton gins of today still operate on the same basic principle as the original, though they are much faster.

Eli Whitney established a plant for manufacturing cotton gins in New Haven, Connecticut. However, he was unable to remain in business and his plant was taken over by others.



**Model of the cotton gin, showing how seeds are separated from raw cotton.**
*(The Smithsonian Institution)*

## PAPER

The early people of the world searched for hundreds of years to find something on which they could draw pictures or write messages. They used blocks of clay, sheets of metal, and other substances. Then the ancient Egyptians found a way to make thin sheets from strips of the papyrus plant. The word "paper" came from the name of this plant. Another substance used to write on was the skin of young sheep or goats; this was called "parchment."

The Chinese finally came up with something better around A.D. 105, when a man named Ts'ai Lun mixed the inner fibers of mulberry bark, hemp, and cloth with water, mashed them to a pulp, pressed out the liquid, and hung the sheets out to dry. This was the first paper as we know it today.

Papermaking was unknown outside the Orient until around A.D. 800, when the Caliph of Baghdad brought Chinese papermakers all the way from their native land. Almost 350 years elapsed before the craft of papermaking spread to Europe. However, part of the secret had been lost – the part about using the fibers of the mulberry tree.

All paper made in the Western world was produced from cotton and linen fibers. Then, in 1719, a Frenchman named René de Réaumur discovered that wood could also be used. But despite this rediscovery of an ancient secret, the process of making paper was still a slow and tedious job, with the sheets being made one at a time by hand.

In 1798 another Frenchman, Nicholas Robert, invented a machine to make paper. He tried to sell his machine to papermakers, but it had not been developed enough to be practical. The rights for the machine were finally acquired by the English brothers Henry and Sealy Fourdrinier, and they lost all their money trying to improve it. However, papermaking machines are still called Fourdriniers in honor of the brothers.

Papermaking is now one of the most important industries in the world. The paper industry in the United States alone requires seventy million tons of wood each year, which is enough logs to extend into space eight times as far away as the moon!



**Before the invention of the Fourdrinier, paper was made one sheet at a time.**
*(The Smithsonian Institution)*

# STEAMBOAT

Well before James Watt developed the first practical steam engine, ingenious men had tried to propel boats by steam. However, it was not until nearly forty years after Watt's engine appeared that a steamboat passed the test of commercial service. The man who designed this first practical steamboat, and who became known as the father of steam navigation, was an American named Robert Fulton.

The son of an Irish immigrant, Robert Fulton was born in Lancaster County, Pennsylvania, in 1765. At the age of fourteen he displayed his inventive genius when he devised a mechanism for propelling boats by paddle wheels. When he was twenty-two he went to Europe, where he studied painting and continued his career as an inventor. Among others, he invented machines for sawing marble, spinning flax, and twisting hemp into rope. He also developed workable submarines for the French and British and conducted tests with a boat powered by steam.

Fulton returned to New York in 1806, when he again took up the challenge of steam navigation. A shipbuilder supplied a vessel 131 feet long and about 20 feet wide, with a displacement of 160 tons. A pair of paddle wheels on the sides were attached to an engine built in England to the inventor's specifications. This engine had a single cylinder two feet in diameter.

Robert Fulton's distinctive achievement was not in inventing either the engine or the boat, but in calculating the total work to be done by the engine, the effectiveness of paddle wheels of various types, and the resistance of the hull in the water.

Fulton announced a trial of his *Clermont* on August 17, 1807. A crowd gathered on the banks of the Hudson River to watch. Smoke poured from the stack and the boat moved slowly forward, then stopped. In a short time Fulton had his engine running again and traveled 150 miles upstream to Albany in thirty-two hours. Regular passenger trips, begun a few days later, convinced the most skeptical that steam navigation had become a reality.



**A drawing of the *Clermont* during its first trials on August 17, 1807.**
***(The Smithsonian Institution)***

NORTH RIVER
of
CLERMONT

# LOCOMOTIVE

The era of the steam locomotive has virtually ended in developed sections of the world. Lighter, more efficient, and much cleaner forms of power have been invented to replace the puffing steam engines. However, the old iron horse must go down as one of the most useful inventions ever conceived by men of vision.

Richard Trevithick of England became interested in the possibility of steam for locomotion, and in 1803 he completed his first machine, which was a big steam boiler set on wheels. It was not very practical and could only creep over muddy or rutted roads. This gave him the idea of laying rails for his machine to run on. Three years later he had made the first true steam locomotive, which could go about five miles per hour over level ground.

Trevithick had made the first step, but his design was not practical enough to be successful. Most of the problems of steam locomotion were finally worked out by another Englishman, George Stephenson. After years of study and experiment, he persuaded the owners of a coal mine to allow him to build a machine which he called a "traveling engine," to haul coal from the mines. His first locomotive began pulling cars of coal on July 25, 1814.

Stephenson opened the first passenger railroad in 1825. Five years later tracks had been laid between Liverpool and Manchester. Stephenson had also improved his original design so much that his new locomotive, called the *Rocket,* could attain a speed of twenty-nine miles per hour.

But while the British had invented the locomotive, it was the Americans who made the greatest advancements in railroad engineering.

By 1860 American locomotives were bigger, more powerful, and much faster than any others. And whereas the British system of tracks was complicated and expensive, an American named Robert Stevens invented the method of using wooden ties and T-shaped rails and hook-headed spikes. These innovations made railroad travel much more comfortable for passengers.



**The *Tom Thumb* was the first U.S.-built locomotive on a commercial railroad.**
***(The Baltimore & Ohio Railroad Co.)***

PETER COOPER'S "TOM THUMB" 1829-30 BALTIMORE & OHIO R.R.

## ELECTRIC GENERATOR

The strange phenomenon of electricity had been known for approximately 2,400 years before anyone knew exactly what it was or how it could be used. Many people experimented with this mysterious force—among them Benjamin Franklin—but it seemed to have no practical use other than for parlor games.

Then, in 1780, an Italian scientist named Alessandro Volta discovered that he could produce electricity by immersing sheets of copper and zinc in a solution of salt water. This was the world's first battery.

Men had known for about two thousand years that certain rocks found in a section of Greece called Magnesia would pick up small iron particles. These stones were called "magnets," after the place where they were discovered. Scientists could not understand why these particular stones had such unusual properties.

The first answer to this question came in 1822 when André Ampère in France made the discovery that a coil of wire with electricity flowing through it acted just like a magnet. He also found that by inserting a piece of soft iron into his coil he could turn the iron into a magnet. These were simple discoveries, but they opened the world to electrical research.

In 1823 an Englishman named William Sturgeon bent an iron bar into the shape of a horseshoe and, by wrapping thin wire around it and applying electrical current, developed the first electromagnet. Then an American, Joseph Henry, learned how to insulate wire and made an electromagnet capable of lifting 750 pounds.

Shortly after this, Henry in the United States and Michael Faraday in England asked themselves the same question: if electricity could produce magnetism, might not magnetism produce electricity? These men, working independently and unaware of each other, produced the first generators in 1831. Nearly forty years passed before Zénobe Gramme, a Belgian, used the principles of these first generators to produce electricity cheaply and efficiently, thus making this power available to industry.



**Joseph Henry's first electromagnet was small but could lift nine pounds.**
*(The Smithsonian Institution)*

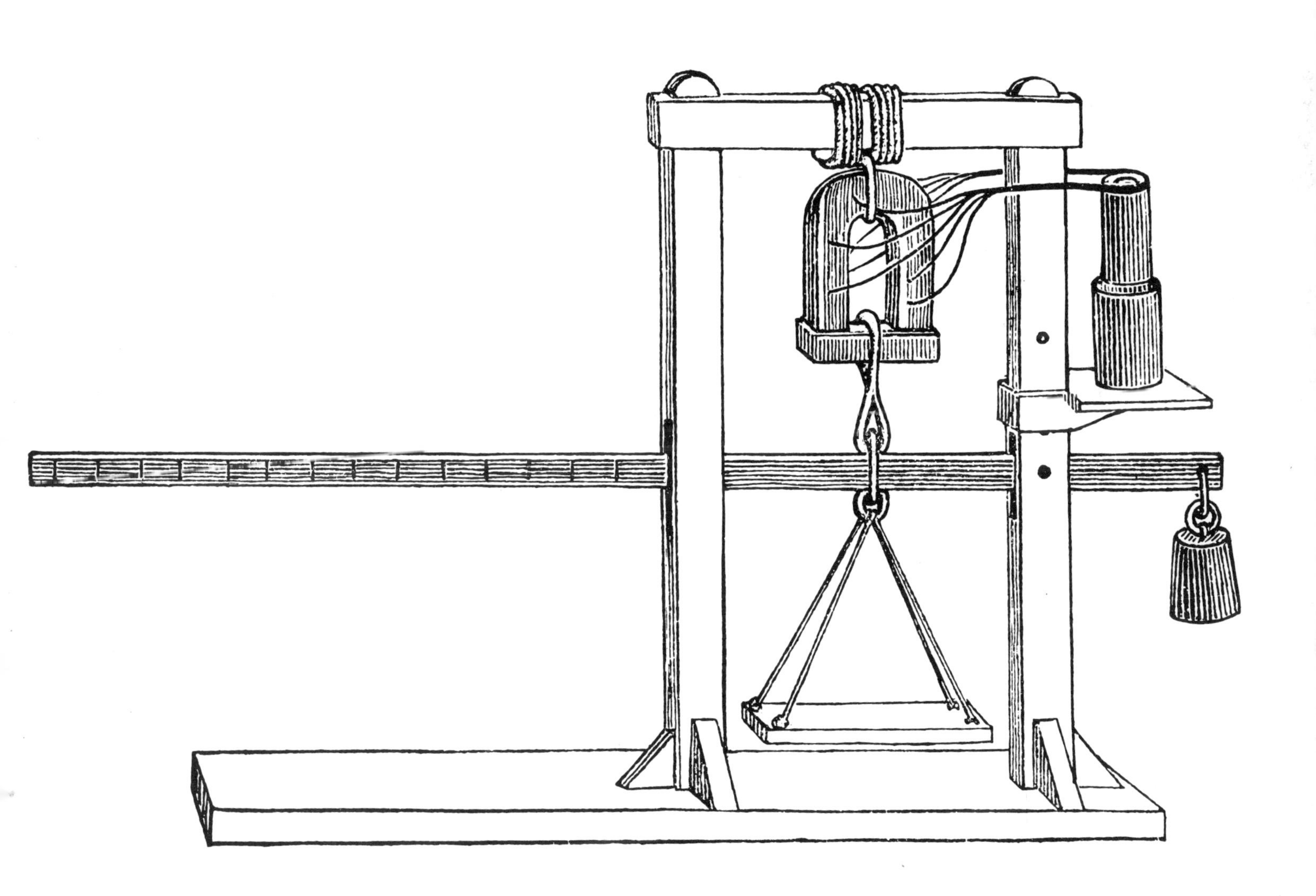

# TELEGRAPH

As with Robert Fulton, Samuel Morse shifted a powerful creative talent from art to science. The result was a new means of communication capable of spanning a continent or an ocean, almost with the speed of thought.

Born in Charlestown, Massachusetts, in 1791, Morse was educated at Yale and then studied painting in England. Before he was twenty-five, his works were hung in the Royal Academy in London. His paintings are still considered to be outstanding examples of early American art.

In 1832, when Morse was forty-one years old, he thought that if electricity could travel any distance over a wire, it might be made to transmit messages. During the next six years he devoted nearly all his time and money in an effort to devise an instrument capable of sending and receiving messages in a code he had devised.

Morse's idea was simple. It allowed electricity to pass along a wire in a series of pulses, which were recorded on paper at the other end of the wire through use of a pencil operated by an electromagnet. The pencil recorded his code as a series of dots and dashes, which could be read back by an operator as letters and words.

Morse demonstrated his telegraph in 1836. A man named Alfred Vail offered financial assistance and also discovered that it was possible to distinguish the dots and dashes by sound alone. This made the recording pencil unnecessary.

The U. S. Government became interested in the telegraph and appropriated $30,000 for construction of a telegraph line between Washington and Baltimore, Maryland, a distance of forty miles. The line was finally installed, and on May 24, 1844, Morse sent these words as the first message: "What hath God wrought?"

Telegraph lines were soon strung in every direction, in the United States as well as in Europe. An underwater cable was laid between England and France in 1850, and in 1866 the first cable was laid across the Atlantic Ocean between the United States and England.



**Samuel Morse sending his first telegram over the Baltimore-Washington line.**
*(The Western Union Telegraph Co.)*

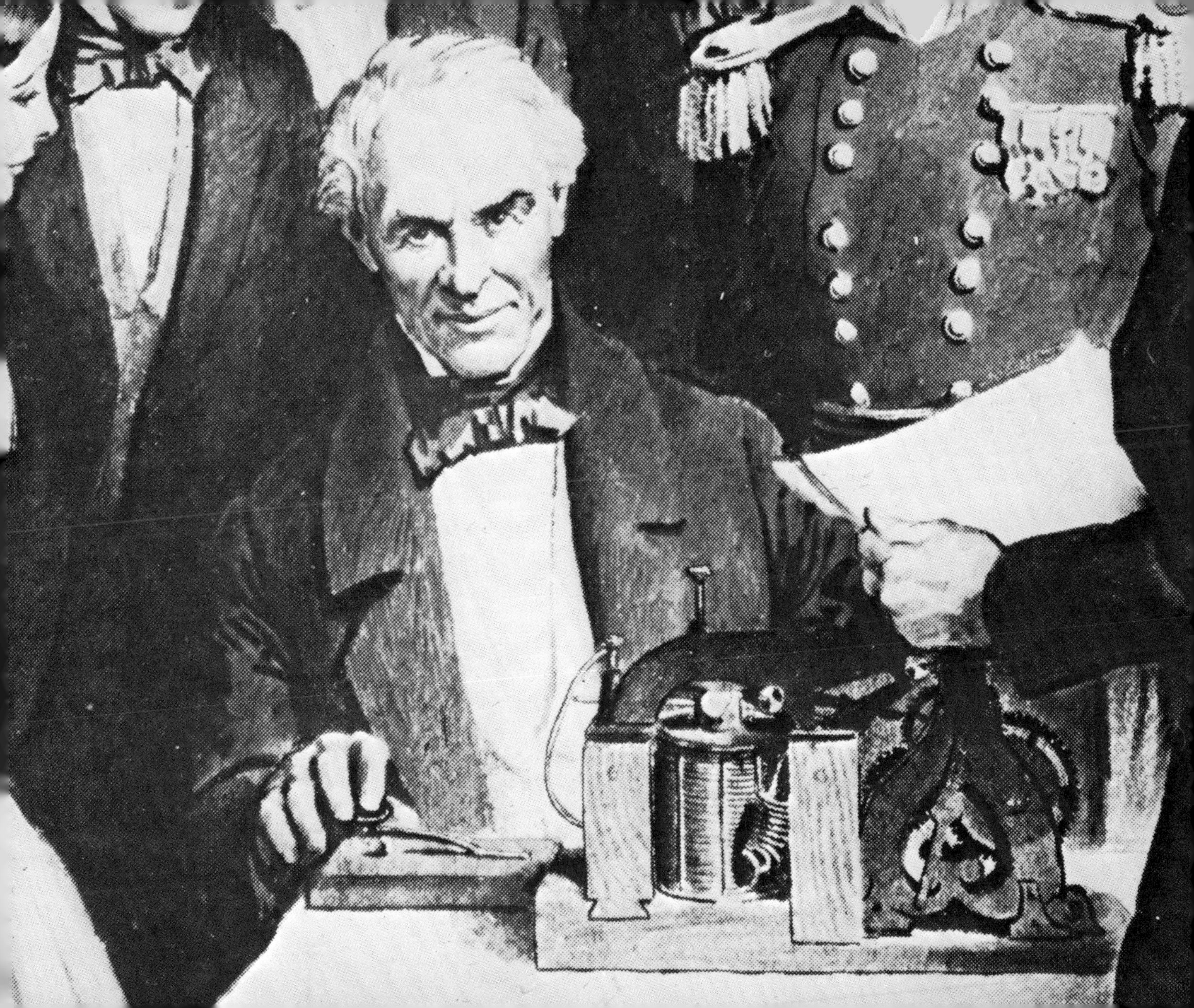

## RUBBER

In 1736 a Frenchman named Charles de la Condamine returned to Paris after exploring the jungles of Peru. He brought with him samples of a soft, spongy substance which he called *caoutchouc*, saying that it was made from the sap of certain trees which grew wild in Peru.

No one knew what to do with this peculiar substance. In the winter it became hard as a stone, and in the summer it became sticky and had a terrible odor. Then an Englishman found that it could be used to rub out mistakes in penciled writing. After this discovery, people started calling the substance "rubber."

Some businessmen found that rubber—or India rubber, as it became known—could be thinned down with turpentine. Charles Macintosh in England used this liquid to make coats waterproof. Other businessmen used it to make boots, hats, and other things. However, it still turned hard in winter and sticky and smelly in summer.

Charles Goodyear in the United States became interested in rubber in 1834. He was not a scientist, but he felt he might be able to turn rubber into something useful. He tried mixing it with everything imaginable—salt, sugar, pepper, castor oil. Nothing worked, but Goodyear still felt he would finally discover a way to cure rubber.

Charles Goodyear was a poor man. Once a person looking for him was told: "If you see a man with an India-rubber coat, India-rubber shoes, an India-rubber hat, and in his pocket an India-rubber purse without a cent in it, that would be Charles Goodyear."

Goodyear had failure after failure. Then, in 1839, he made a great discovery. He had mixed sulphur with some of his raw rubber and accidentally dropped it on a hot stove. Rather than melting, this sample became hard and firm. By accident, he had learned the secret of "vulcanization"—that rubber mixed with sulphur, and then heated, would become durable, remaining soft and pliable in any weather.

Goodyear did not invent rubber, but he did find a way to turn it into a useful commodity and create a huge new industry.



**Charles Goodyear learned how to vulcanize rubber in the winter of 1839.**
*(The Goodyear Tire & Rubber Co.)*

GEORGE RAPP

# SEWING MACHINE

The sewing machine has found its way to more remote areas of the world than any other machine invented by man. It has been a blessing to millions of women and has raised standards of living by making possible rapid factory production of low-cost clothing.

A British inventor named Thomas Saint made the first known sewing machine in 1780. It used a single strand of thread and formed a chain stitch. However, this stitch unraveled if the thread was broken. His machine was practical for sewing leather and other heavy material, but not for clothing.

The first lockstitch machine using two threads was invented by Walter Hunt, an American, around 1832. Hunt abandoned his device for fear that it would put tailors and seamstresses out of work.

Meanwhile, another American, Elias Howe, overheard a clothing maker complain that a practical sewing machine was not yet available. Howe was a poor man, with a wife and three children to support, but he spent all his spare time during the next five years in an effort to develop such a machine. He used the two-thread, lockstitch principle, and was finally granted a patent for his device in 1846. In a demonstration, Howe's machine was pitted against five seamstresses sewing by hand. His machine sewed faster and better than the combined output of the experienced women.

American clothing makers, unfortunately, did not immediately recognize the merits of the sewing machine. In annoyance, Howe went to England and sold the British rights to his invention for $1,250.

The demand for sewing machines started slowly, then suddenly soared. By 1860, more machines were being sold in Europe than in the United States. And surprisingly, seamstresses were not put out of work. Instead, much more labor was needed in the factories to meet the increased demand for low-cost clothing.

The sewing machine proved such a boon that one nineteenth-century editor described it as "next to the plow, humanity's most blessed instrument."



**Elias Howe's first successful sewing machine, with wooden carrying case.**
***(The Smithsonian Institution)***

# REAPER

Visitors to the 1851 industrial exposition in London stared with wonder and some amusement as a strange machine was set in place in the American section. The mechanical freak was a reaper, which had been invented by Cyrus McCormick. It was a horse-drawn implement designed to cut grain more quickly than the ancient scythe or the more modern cradle—both of which were hand-operated instruments.

When the reaper was tested in a field near London, about 200 curious farmers gathered. They were amazed when the machine, pulled by two horses, cut a swath about 220 feet long through the green, heavy wheat in seventy seconds. Returned to the exhibition hall, the reaper became the center of attention. The London *Times* called it "the most valuable contribution from abroad."

Cyrus McCormick was a farmer in Walnut Grove, Virginia, where he was born in 1809. As a boy, he had swung the heavy cradle in his father's fields. This implement cut much faster than the scythe, but McCormick dreamed of a machine that would cut swiftly without shaking the grain from the stalks. He made his first reaper in 1831 and improved it in succeeding years. Working with a cradle, it had required three days for a man to cut four acres of wheat; McCormick's earliest machines could reap more than six acres a day. By the 1850's he had so improved his reaper that it cut at the rate of about an acre every forty minutes, which just a few years previously would have been considered impossible.

McCormick's was not the first reaper. Other inventors had patented machines before 1831 in Europe as well as in the United States. However, McCormick had solved problems of design which no one else had overcome.

The reaper worked radical changes in agriculture. As late as the 1850's, the United States was forced to import wheat while grain rotted on farms for lack of men to cut and gather it. Within a short time Cyrus McCormick's invention turned the United States into a rich land of agricultural abundance.



**The reaper invented by McCormick brought about a revolution in farming.**
*(International Harvester Co.)*

## TYPEWRITER

The first known inventor of a writing machine was a British engineer named Henry Mill, who received a patent on his device in 1714. The patent described the invention as "an Artificial Machine or Method for the Impressing or Transcribing of Letters Singly or Progressively one after another, as in Writing, whereby all Writing whatever may be Engrossed in Paper or Parchment so Neat and Exact as not to be distinguished from Print." There is no record that this machine was ever actually produced.

Other men attempted to make machines capable of typing on paper, one of whom was an American named Austin Burt, who received a patent for his device in 1829. However, all details of the Burt machine are lacking since these were destroyed by a fire in the patent office.

A magazine article about these early machines intrigued Christopher L. Sholes, the collector of customs at Milwaukee, Wisconsin, and he decided to try to invent a writing machine.

With the assistance of two friends, Sholes produced his first typewriter in 1867. This simple machine used a telegraph key linked to a pivot arm and printed a single character, the letter W. A few months later he had a working model with a complete alphabet as well as numerals.

After making a total of thirty different models, Sholes and his friends patented their first practical typewriter in 1873. The following year it was put into production by E. Remington and Sons, makers of sewing machines, firearms, and farm machinery.

This first typewriter looked strange by comparison with modern machines. However, even the most advanced models of today work on the exact same principle as the Sholes machine.

In 1881 a school in New York offered to teach young women how to use the typewriter. Then, suddenly, businessmen awoke to the advantages of a machine that could write sixty or more words per minute. This not only created a demand for typewriters but opened a new career for women in office work.



**The original working model of the Sholes typewriter was built in 1867.**
***(The Smithsonian Institution)***

# TELEPHONE

In 1876 the United States celebrated 100 years of independence with a huge exhibition in Philadelphia. A small space in the section devoted to new inventions had been reserved by a young teacher of elocution named Alexander Graham Bell.

Bell had made an instrument for transmitting the human voice. When the exhibition judges arrived, Bell asked them to listen at a receiving horn, while he spoke into a mouthpiece some distance away. The judges were startled to hear his words come through distinctly.

Born in Scotland in 1847, Alexander Bell emigrated to the United States when he was twenty-four and opened a school for speech training for deaf mutes in Boston. During his spare time Bell studied the human ear, and he concluded that sounds might be transmitted by a continuous electric current, varied in intensity, just as the eardrum responds to changes in the density of the air caused by sound vibrations.

In 1875 Bell learned how to make current fluctuate over a wire. When a reed on his "harmonic telegraph" became stuck and his assistant accidentally touched the other reeds, Bell heard sounds in the receiver. Excited by his discovery, he substituted a tiny drumhead, or diaphragm, for the reed. When the device was tested, he had a working, though primitive, telephone capable of sending and receiving sounds.

The first known person to indicate the possibility of electric telephony was a Frenchman named Charles Bourseul, who in 1854 suggested that sounds could be sent over a wire by making and breaking an electric circuit. However, Bourseul never devised a working instrument. Then, in 1860, Philipp Reis of Germany made an instrument which transmitted sounds, but he discontinued experiments before attaining true success.

Alexander Graham Bell's telephone was the first practical instrument ever devised to transmit and receive the human voice with all its natural quality, and it was destined to become one of the most useful inventions of all time, adding a new dimension to communication.



**The transmitter *(left)* and receiver *(right)* of Bell's first telephone.**
***(American Telephone & Telegraph Co.)***

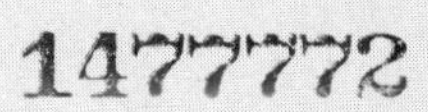
1477772

# PHONOGRAPH

It was a simple machine, but few people could have guessed its function. It consisted of a cylinder, turned by a hand crank and covered with a sheet of tinfoil; it also had a mouthpiece and a sharp metal stylus pointed at the cylinder. The inventor of the device turned the crank as he spoke into the mouthpiece: "Mary had a little lamb." To the surprise of the spectators, the same words were repeated through the mouthpiece when the stylus was put back to the starting point and the crank turned again.

This was the first public demonstration of the phonograph, which was born from the inspiration of America's most amazing inventor, Thomas Alva Edison. Before he died in 1931, Edison had received patents for more than a thousand inventions. He once listed the phonograph as one of his favorite inventions.

Thomas Edison was born in Milan, Ohio, in 1847. He attended school for only three years, but he taught himself both chemistry and electricity. While working as a telegraph operator, he made his first important invention: an instrument which repeated messages over a second line without the presence of an operator. With the money earned from this invention, he set up a laboratory in New Jersey.

There, in 1877, while Edison was testing a telegraphic instrument, an incoming signal caused a needle to vibrate and scratch a pattern on a revolving paper disc. When Edison returned the needle to its starting position and revolved the paper, he heard an odd sound. This made him think that if the vibrations of the human voice were impressed into the proper surface, these might be reproduced to recreate the original sounds. The phonograph was the result.

Until the invention of the phonograph, it had been impossible to record the human voice or any other sound. Thomas Edison's marvelous invention, when perfected, was destined to become a boon to mankind. His phonograph, in its original form, is now known as the Dictaphone, which is used in many large business offices in place of stenographers.



**Thomas Edison making the first public demonstration of his phonograph.**
***(Courtesy of Con Edison, New York)***

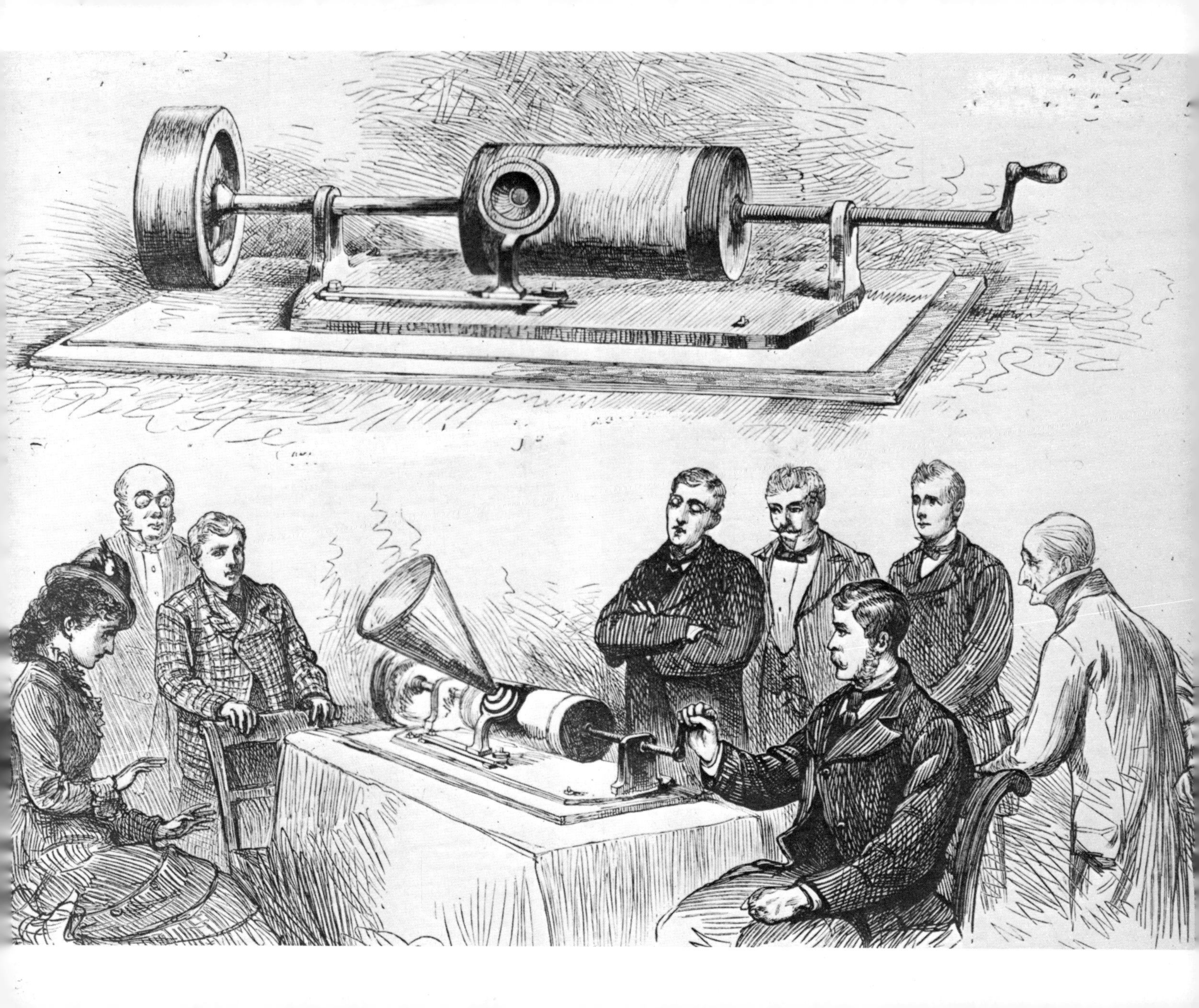

# ELECTRIC LIGHT

For years men had tried to perfect the electric light, and some came close to success. In 1878 Thomas Edison was attracted to the problem. But first he made a thorough study of the gas industry. People were using gas to light their homes, and Edison knew that the electric light would not be accepted unless it was better than gas and also reasonable to operate.

Before going to work on his incandescent bulb, Edison also designed a central power system, since he realized that there would have to be a constant flow of electricity for his bulbs to burn.

With these problems solved, Edison finally turned to the problem of the electric light itself.

Other pioneers had laid the groundwork. One of these was Sir Humphry Davy, an Englishman, who had made a carbon arc lamp. However, this operated on batteries and would burn only a few hours. Then, in 1840, Sir William Groves, another Englishman, made an electric light with a piece of platinum wire as filament. This was unsatisfactory, since fluctuations in current burned out the filament and because the bulb lasted but a few hours.

Edison's first lamp had a platinum filament, but he found that this was not practical. Then he had an idea.

Years previously, while working with a battery, he noted that a piece of paper he had baked in a furnace glowed white-hot before falling into dust. This made him think that a filament of carbon might be the right answer to the problem.

He made a lamp of baked sewing thread and created a vacuum within his bulb so that the filament would not be exposed to oxygen. This seemed to be the right track, for his bulb gave light for forty hours before it burned out.

Edison experimented with six thousand types of filaments to find something better. Of these, bamboo fiber proved the best, and he was granted a patent for his electric light on January 27, 1880. The American inventive genius had succeeded where all others had failed.



**Edison and his staff testing the first successful incandescent lamp.**
***(Courtesy of Con Edison, New York)***

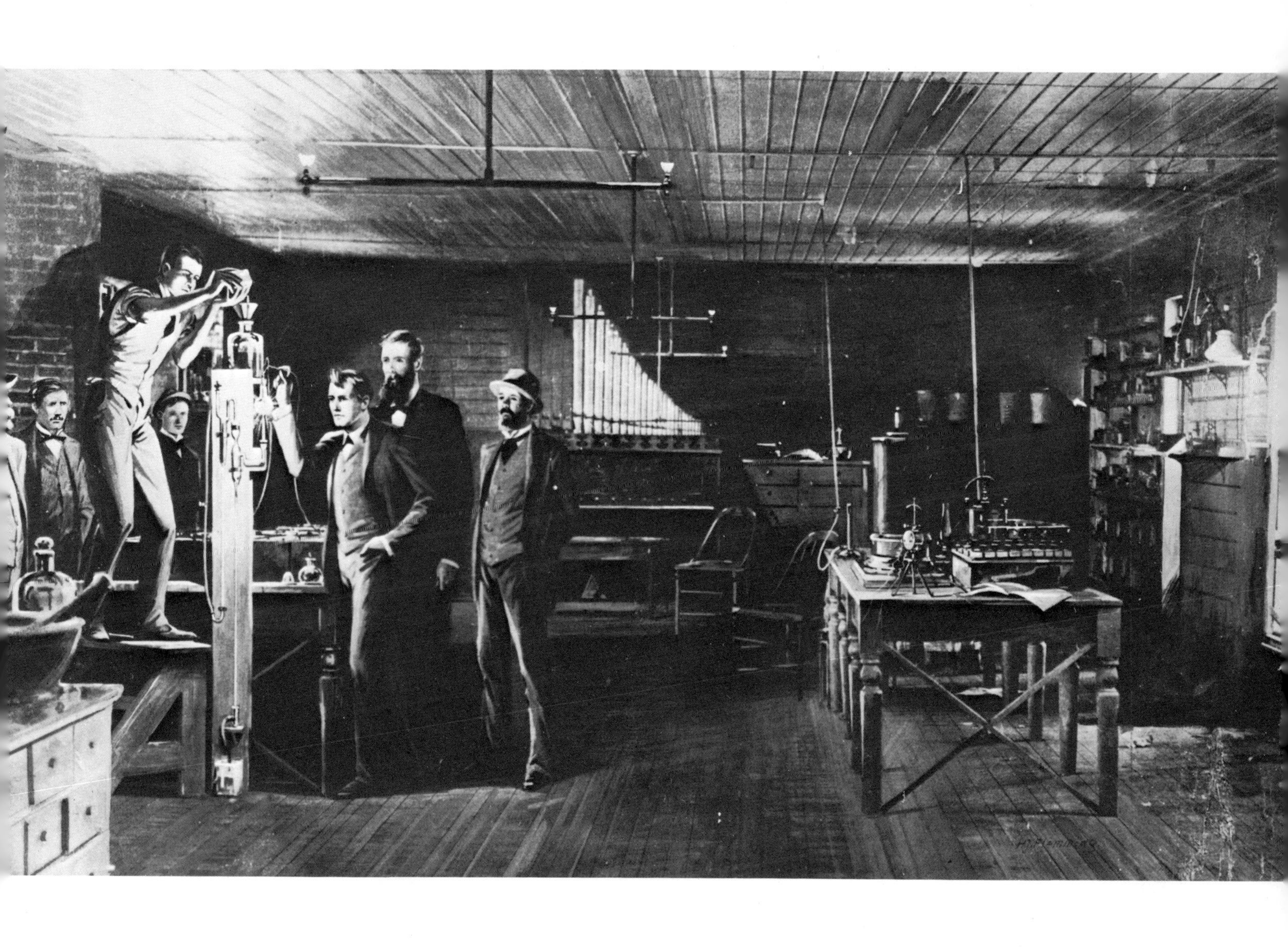

# LINOTYPE

The New York *Tribune* of the 1880's was one of the best and most progressive daily newspapers in the United States. Its staff gathered news quickly over the newly invented telephone and telegraph, wrote it on the still-novel typewriter, and printed it on the most advanced printing presses. However, it was forced to set every line of type by hand, just as printers had done for more than 300 years. This was a slow process and required a large staff of compositors.

Various men had attempted to invent mechanical typesetters, but most of these had too many drawbacks. One such inventor brought his machine to the Baltimore shop of a company which made scientific instruments. A worker in the shop named Ottmar Mergenthaler, who had been born in Germany, saw the machine and decided to make a typesetter of his own design.

Mergenthaler was not a printer, but he studied the craft and discovered what was needed. He then set about designing a machine which would cast a full line of type in a single slug of metal. Because of the operation of his machine, Mergenthaler referred to it as a Linotype.

Mergenthaler's first machine was awkward and not really useful. But after several years of work he perfected a design so efficient that it remains basically the same today. The compositor pressed keys, similar to those on a typewriter. This caused permanent metal molds, one for each letter or numeral, to drop into a line. Molten metal was then forced into the molds, where it hardened at once to form a line of type. Mergenthaler also devised a way of spacing words automatically so that every line of printing could be made the same length.

The New York *Tribune* showed interest in the Linotype, and the first one was set up in the newspaper's composing room in July 1886. Tests showed that the machine was about six times as fast as a man setting type by hand.

Ottmar Mergenthaler's Linotype machine is credited with bringing about the greatest revolution in printing since the invention of the craft.



**Mergenthaler's original Linotype, which was used by the New York *Tribune*.**
***(Mergenthaler Linotype Co.)***

# AUTOMOBILE

The word "automobile" is a combination of the Greek *autos*, which means "self," and the Latin *mobilis*, which means "movable." Together, they mean "self-movable."

For centuries man had depended upon animals for overland travel, but this means of transportation fell far short of actual needs. Something faster and more efficient was desired. However, this had to wait until the development of a device capable of delivering power over an extended period of time and with continued reliability.

After the invention of the steam engine, a number of men attempted to harness this engine to a vehicle. The first successful steam-driven contraption was a three-wheeled monster built in France in 1770 by Nicolas Cugnot. His machine had a huge boiler and steam engine forward of the front wheel; it traveled at a speed of only two miles per hour. Obviously, something better was needed if such a machine was ever to become practical.

The steam engine in its early stage of development was hardly the answer to successful automotive transportation. With this realization, many inventors turned their attention to designing an internal-combustion engine. The first one was developed by a Frenchman, Jean Joseph Lenoir, in 1860. It had a single cylinder and burned illuminating gas. In 1863 Lenoir used his engine to power a crude vehicle which he drove a distance of six miles in one and a half hours.

The first gasoline engine was made by a German, Nikolaus Otto, in 1876. However, he did not attempt to use his engine in a vehicle. Otto's chief engineer, Gottlieb Daimler, continued experiments and in 1885 patented his own gasoline-powered engine, which was an improvement over the Otto design.

Daimler built his first automobile in 1887. Around the same time another German engineer, Karl Benz, also developed a gasoline-powered vehicle, with an engine considerably improved over the Daimler design. These two men later went into business to build Daimler-Benz automobiles, and they generally share credit for development of the "horseless carriage."



**The first Benz automobile, a three-wheeler, appeared in Germany in 1887.**
*(Mercedes-Benz of North America)*

# PHOTOGRAPHY

Photography evolved slowly from an imperfect beginning to the state of reliability and dependability it has reached in modern times, with each step resulting in dramatic improvements.

Early scientists had known that a compound called silver nitrate turned dark when exposed to light, but they did not realize the possibilities of this color change. Then, in 1802, two British scientists, Thomas Wedgewood and Sir Humphry Davy, reasoned that they might be able to use silver nitrate to capture images on paper. Their reasoning was good, but the pictures they took were not permanent and continued to turn darker and darker.

In 1822 a Frenchman, Joseph Niepce, made the first photographs which would not fade, but these had to be exposed for twelve hours. Then in 1839 another Frenchman, Louis Daguerre, invented the first practical method of photography. Daguerreotype photography produced a good picture in just a few minutes. However, there was no negative with this process and so it was not possible to make duplicate prints. This problem was finally solved in 1840 by William Talbot, an Englishman.

Other developments were made in photography through the years, but the greatest advance was by George Eastman, an American. Prior to Eastman's development of flexible film in 1884, all pictures were taken on glass plates. With this invention, photography became practical as a hobby for the average person with a small camera instead of a profession for a photographer with a bulky camera.

Still another great advance was the invention of the Polaroid Land camera in 1949 by Edwin Land, an American. This remarkable process gives a picture in just a few seconds without need of a negative.

Color photography has also had a long history of development. However, this did not become truly practical for the average amateur photographer until Kodak, the company started by George Eastman, introduced their Kodachrome film in 1935. This opened a new field for photographic reality.



**Photography required bulky equipment before Eastman produced flexible film.**
***(The Smithsonian Institution)***

# ELECTRIC POWER SYSTEM

Even before Samuel Morse sent his first feeble telegraph signals over a wire with battery current, other experimenters were seeking a more powerful source of electricity. They reasoned that if a sufficiently strong charge could be produced, it might be "piped" into homes and workshops to provide light, heat, and power. Among the talented men who helped put electricity to work, none surpassed the achievements of Nikola Tesla.

Tesla was born in Austria-Hungary in 1857. As a student he saw the dynamo invented by Zénobe Gramme of Belgium, and he conceived an idea for a generator based on an entirely different principle. He came to the United States in 1884 to work in Thomas Edison's laboratory. The inventor recognized Tesla's ability, but the two men differed over the best way to generate and transmit electric power.

Edison had built the world's first central power station in New York City. The station produced direct current, but there were many drawbacks to the system. Tesla recognized the problems and invented a generator which produced alternating current – electric power which changed its direction of flow, or polarity, many times per second. He proved that this current could be transmitted at a higher voltage than direct current, then stepped down to a safe level before it entered the lines of the consumer. The argument over the best type of electrical system caused Edison and Tesla to part.

In May 1888 the young inventor was invited to explain his system before the American Institute of Electrical Engineers. George Westinghouse, who had prospered from his invention of the railroad air brake, financed the Tesla enterprises. In 1891 the two men were instrumental in constructing a hydroelectric plant at Niagara Falls. The tremendous power of the falls was harnessed to ten giant turbines. Within a few years electricity was flowing to the homes and factories of Buffalo, New York, some twenty-two miles away.

Today, every power station may well be looked upon as a monument to the genius of Nikola Tesla.



**Interior of the Niagara Falls power station, with three of the turbines.**
*(The Smithsonian Institution)*

# X RAY

In 1858 a German physicist named Julius Plücker made a peculiar discovery. He played a high-voltage electric spark on a glass tube from which most of the air had been removed, and was surprised to see the tube glow with a bright purplish light. Other scientists found that as more air was removed from a tube, the glow first brightened and then disappeared completely. The glow was said to be caused by "cathode rays" generated in the vacuum tube.

In November 1895 Wilhelm Roentgen, a professor of physics in Wurzburg, Germany, conducted experiments with a cathode-ray tube. He enclosed a tube in a lightproof black cardboard box and screened out all light from his laboratory.

Roentgen noticed something peculiar every time he shot an electrical charge into the tube. There was no visible light from the tube, but an eerie glow appeared on his nearby workbench. The glow came from a piece of paper he had coated with a substance called platinocyanide.

Excited by his discovery, he found that the paper continued to glow no matter what he placed between it and the tube. On one test the paper became bright even when he placed a thick book between it and the cathode-ray tube.

Roentgen concluded that the tube was emitting some sort of powerful rays. He didn't know what they were, and he wrote, "To distinguish these from other rays I will call them 'X rays.'"

The scientist became more excited when he found that the bones in his hand cast shadows on the paper, while the rays passed easily through his flesh.

Wilhelm Roentgen had discovered one of the most powerful tools in mankind's quest for knowledge. For the first time, it became possible to look into the human body without surgery. Other uses were also found for these amazing rays, including study of the structure of the atom.

Roentgen had been experimenting in the dark that day in his laboratory, but his discovery was to light a new path to scientific exploration.



**Roentgen astounded scientists at his first demonstration of X rays in 1896.**

# SUBMARINE

As with so many other inventions, it is difficult to attribute the development of the submarine to any one man. Several inventors attempted to design and build underwater vessels, with varying degrees of success.

As early as 1620 a Dutch physician, Cornelis van Drebbel, was said to have made two fully enclosed boats fitted with oars. It is also claimed that underwater voyages were made with his vessels. However, this seems doubtful.

The first submersible vessel that came anything near success was one built by David Bushnell, an American. Bushnell called his craft the *Turtle*, and on September 6, 1776, during the War of Independence, it was used to attack the British warship *Eagle*. The *Turtle* operated well, but the attack was not successful.

Robert Fulton, who later became famous for his steamship, next tried his hand at the submarine. He made his first one for the French government in 1801, and his second for the British in 1805. However, the British were so concerned by the war potentials of the submarine that they offered Fulton a large sum of money to discontinue his experiments.

During the American Civil War the Confederate *Hunley* became the first submarine to sink an enemy warship, the Union *Housatonic*. This battle took place on February 17, 1864, in the harbor of Charleston, South Carolina. The *Hunley* and its crew were also lost in the action.

The world's first practical submarine, and the first to be commissioned by the U. S. Navy, was the *Holland*, which was designed by John P. Holland and delivered for service on April 11, 1900.

While the *Holland* was able to travel submerged, it was not considered a true submarine, since it had to surface to charge its batteries. The world's first true submarine was the *Nautilus*, which was commissioned by the U. S. Navy on September 30, 1954. Powered by atomic fuel, the *Nautilus* could remain submerged almost indefinitely since there were no batteries to be charged.



**The *Holland* was delivered to the U. S. Navy for service on April 11, 1900.**
*(General Dynamics Corp.)*

HOLLAND

# AIRPLANE

Most Americans generally accept the fact that Wilbur and Orville Wright of Dayton, Ohio, were not only the first men to fly in a heavier-than-air machine but the inventors of the airplane. This same view is not always shared by historians—not because of new evidence, but from reexamination of the old.

According to the Wright brothers, five persons besides themselves were present at Kitty Hawk, North Carolina, when they flew for the first time on December 17, 1903. They claimed that they flew four times that day, and that the last flight covered 852 feet in 59 seconds. The skeptics insist that this would have required an air speed of about 37 miles per hour with the stiff headwinds which were blowing that day, and that this speed probably could not have been realized with a thirteen-horsepower engine. Six years later Glenn Curtiss won the First International Air Meet with a speed of only 47.6 miles per hour.

Two other people claimed that they flew well before the Wrights. One of these was a Frenchman, Clément Ader, who said he managed to become airborne from a field near Paris on October 9, 1890—and with four witnesses. Another American, Gustave Whitehead, insisted that he flew successfully in 1899, 1901, and again in 1902. A newspaperman named Richard Howell even wrote an account of an alleged flight by Whitehead on August 14, 1901.

Despite these claims, there is no doubt that the Wrights were the first aeronautical engineers if not indeed the first to fly. One problem that had dogged earlier pioneers was that of keeping the wings level. The Wrights solved this by warping the trailing

Before building their first airplane, the Wrights tested more than 200 miniature wing shapes in their wind tunnel, then tried the best ones in glider flight. They made between 700 and 1,000 glider flights in one period of only two months.

The questions of who really invented the airplane and flew for the first time will probably never be answered. However, all of the pioneers, including those who failed, deserve shared credit.



Orville Wright flying at Kitty Hawk while his brother Wilbur watches.
*(U. S. Air Force)*

# RADIO

Today we look upon the radio as an accepted means of communication in our daily lives. However, many people can remember when radio was still considered a strange novelty.

Guglielmo Marconi, an Italian, is generally called the inventor of the radio. The official records state that he invented the system in 1895. But Marconi was only one among the many experimenters in the field, and his contributions the final steps to a science which had begun more than twenty years previously.

The history of the radio actually began in 1873, when an English physicist named James Maxwell published his theory of electromagnetic waves. Maxwell never attempted to prove his theory, but about fifteen years later Heinrich Hertz, a German, managed to generate such waves electrically. For years these were referred to as Hertzian waves rather than as radio waves.

About the same time, a British scientist named David Hughes discovered that a tube containing loosely packed metal particles would conduct electromagnetic waves. He called his tube a "coherer," but he did not develop it further.

Marconi became interested in the possibilities of wireless telegraphy in 1890. His first step was to make an improved coherer in 1894. This tube, with other of his inventions, resulted in the first crude radio. By 1896 Marconi was able to send wireless telegraph signals about a mile. The following year he transmitted signals to a ship at sea eighteen miles away, and in 1899 he established commercial communication between England and France. Two years later his first signals were sent across the Atlantic Ocean to Newfoundland.

Marconi learned how to send signals without wires, but he could not transmit music or the human voice. This development was made by Reginald Fessenden, a Canadian who emigrated to the United States. Fessenden's first radio-telephonic broadcast was made on December 24, 1906. Within a few years, radio broadcasting as we know it today became a reality.



**Reginald Fessenden in his laboratory at Brant Rock, Massachusetts, in 1906.**
*(The Smithsonian Institution)*

# VACUUM TUBE

The vacuum tube is one of the most dynamic devices ever conceived, opening a fresh path to technological progress. It is a vital element in radio and television broadcasting, in long-distance telephony, and in numerous other electronic instruments. These all depend upon the three-element tube, or audion, which was originated in 1906 by Lee De Forest, one of the early experimenters in radio.

As a boy in Council Bluffs, Iowa, where he was born in 1873, De Forest showed a strong scientific interest. He was fifteen years old in 1888 when Heinrich Hertz of Germany discovered the properties of radio waves. Later, as a student at Yale University, De Forest wrote a paper on Hertzian waves. This was considered one of the best reports ever written on the subject.

The three-element vacuum tube was the outgrowth of De Forest's six-year search to find a sensitive detector of radio waves. In 1904 an Englishman named John Fleming made the first vacuum tube, but it fell far short of requirements. De Forest finally evolved a tube which greatly amplified the signals picked up by the Fleming tube. Radio receivers of today usually employ Fleming's tube to detect the signal and De Forest's audion to amplify it. Transistor radios are based on the same working components of these tubes.

De Forest's great advance made practical the transmission of the human voice and music over long distances without the necessity of wires. In 1908 he broadcast phonograph music from the Eiffel Tower in Paris that was heard by radio as far away as Marseilles.

In the 1920's De Forest took up the challenge of making motion pictures talk electronically. He was the first to work out a practical method of representing sound waves as photographic images on the same film that carried the picture. This principle is still used in making sound films.

All modern vacuum tubes retain De Forest's original principle, although extra elements have been added and some tubes have been reduced drastically in size.



**De Forest's vacuum tubes, or audions, were called electronic marvels.**
*(The Smithsonian Institution)*

# ROCKET

There has never been any doubt that the rocket, along with paper, printing, and gunpowder, was a Chinese invention. But there has been much speculation about when the first rockets were made. Some sources claim that these go back to as much as 3,000 years before the birth of Christ, while others insist that the invention must have been made around A.D. 1200. This latter assumption is made since rockets were supposedly used first as war weapons by the Mongols in the year 1232 against the city of Pien-king, which was later renamed Kaifeng.

Rocketry as a true science did not begin until 1895, when a Russian named Konstantin Ziolkovsky suggested that solid fuels would not provide enough power for space travel and that liquid fuels of the kerosene type would be the best answer. About this time a German, Hermann Ganswindt, designed a spaceship which was amazingly advanced for its day. However, neither Ziolkovsky nor Ganswindt ever attempted to prove their theories.

Finally, in 1919, a new era began in rocket research when Dr. Robert Goddard in the United States wrote that it was possible to send a rocket to the moon. Goddard tried unsuccessfully to obtain financial assistance from the government to conduct tests, but unlike others before him, he started practical research with his own money.

Goddard launched his first liquid-fuel rocket on November 1, 1923, and realized a flight of 184 feet. After many tests, he sent one of his rockets to an altitude of 7,500 feet on May 31, 1935.

Meanwhile, as a result of Dr. Goddard's work, the Germans started studying rocketry. These studies, which were financed by the government, resulted in the V-2 rocket of World War II. These were the largest rockets made to that time, measuring 46 feet from nose to tail.

Since the end of the war, rocketry has advanced by leaps and bounds, and it now promises to be one of the greatest inventions that man's ingenuity has ever conceived, opening a vast new world of exploration in outer space.



**Robert Goddard in his workshop with one of his test rockets in 1935.**
*(Esther C. Goddard)*

# RADAR

Until the invention of radar, it was impossible for man to look through the blackness of night or clouds or heavy fog. This caused many problems and dangers. Radar, which means "radio detection and ranging," changed all this. No longer can enemy warships or airplanes strike suddenly without being detected, and no longer do pilots have to worry about what might be on the other side of a cloud or hidden in dense fog.

Radar added many new dimensions to the quest for knowledge, not the least important of which is truly accurate mapping of mountains and coastlines. Without radar it would also be impossible to track rockets in flight to other planets.

Heinrich Hertz had proved in Germany as early as 1888 that radio waves could be reflected back from solid objects. In 1904 Christian Hulsmeyer, another German, thought that radio echoes could be used to aid ship navigation. However, no one tried this idea in practice until 1925, when two Americans, George Breit and Merle Tuve, used radio waves to explore the ionosphere, which is one of the upper layers of the earth's atmosphere. Then an Englishman named Robert Watson-Watt proved that by the use of radio waves airplanes in flight could be detected long before they came into sight. The British Air Ministry conducted further research and in 1935 started work on a chain of radar stations as early warning against possible enemy attack. These radar stations helped the British defeat the German bombers in their wartime raids against London.

Meanwhile, scientists in the United States were continuing research. In 1922 Leo Young and A. Hoyt Taylor, working in the U. S. Naval Research Laboratory, had suggested the possibility of detecting enemy warships by radio waves. By 1933 they had developed an efficient system.

While radar was originally thought of only as a defensive system against attack, its value now seems almost limitless. Coupled with other instruments, it can land airplanes safely without the pilot touching his controls, and the end of its application is still nowhere in sight.



**Early radar equipment developed by Young and Taylor for the U. S. Navy.**
*(The Smithsonian Institution)*

# TELEVISION

The word "television" is a combination of two Greek words which mean "see from far off." It is unquestionably one of the most important inventions of all time, bringing entertainment into the home, accelerating education in some areas of the world, improving manufacturing methods in industry.

While television is generally believed to be a fairly new invention, the basic idea is not new by any means. The first known experiments date back to 1884, when a German named Paul Nipkow tried to perfect a device to send pictures electronically.

Nipkow's invention consisted of a disc with small holes in it from the rim to the center. By revolving the disc rapidly in front of the eye, light would come through the holes to form a picture. By the use of photoelectric cells and lenses, Nipkow was able to send pictures over wires electronically. This was the first real television, but it was not sufficiently clear to be practical.

Primitive forms of wireless television were broadcast experimentally in England in 1927 and in the United States in 1930, but true electronic television had to wait for further advancements.

The first of these was the iconoscope, which was developed in 1933 by an American named Vladimir Zworykin. The iconoscope is a device capable of picking up variations in light intensity and transferring these into variations in electrical charge.

The second development was the electronic television camera, which was invented in 1934 by Philo Farnsworth, another American.

The iconoscope and the electronic camera made commercial television possible, and broadcasting on a scheduled basis began in the United States on April 30, 1939. Service was interrupted by World War II, however, and did not start again until 1946. Today, there are more than 55 million television sets in use by homeowners in the United States alone.

Through special satellites in orbit around the earth, television can now be broadcast to viewers thousands of miles away, thus making the world much smaller.



**Young Philo Farnsworth invented the electronic television camera in 1934.**
***(The Smithsonian Institution)***

# ATOMIC POWER

On December 2, 1942, something utterly fantastic occurred on the squash court under the stadium of Chicago University. There, for the first time in history, human beings produced energy in the same way it is produced in the stars—by atomic fission. Two and a half years later, on July 16, 1945, the world's first atomic bomb was detonated at White Sands, New Mexico, unleashing the greatest amount of power ever generated on earth.

The word "atom" comes from the Greek *atomos*, which means "indivisible." As long ago as 500 B.C., a Greek philosopher named Democritus said that all substance was composed of invisible atoms. He was right, but the name given to this tiny particle was wrong, for scientists now know that atoms can be split, or divided, and that when this occurs a tremendous amount of energy is given off.

The first stumbling steps toward atomic power were made in 1898 by Pierre and Marie Curie in France, when they discovered that uranium ore was unstable and radiated energy. Other scientists theorized that if the uranium atoms could be broken down quickly instead of by natural means, they would give off huge quantities of energy. One of these scientists was named Enrico Fermi, who had been born in Italy but emigrated to the United States in 1938.

Fermi continued to experiment with atoms in the United States. He and another atomic scientist, J. Robert Oppenheimer, were given funds by the U. S. Government so that they could intensify their studies along with a staff of learned men. After spending two billion dollars on the project, they succeeded in producing the first man-made atomic explosion.

While atomic energy was originally produced as the most awesome and horrifying military weapon of all time, men of vision realized that from this destruction could come a new power source of incalculable benefit. For finally man had the power of the universe in his grasp, to be tamed and put to work for the good of all rather than for destruction.



**A drawing of the atomic reactor set up at Chicago University in 1942.**
***(U. S. Atomic Energy Commission)***

# COMPUTER

As long ago as about 600 B.C. the Chinese invented a device called an abacus, which could give the answers to simple mathematical problems much faster than a man working with pencil and paper. The abacus took much of the work out of mathematics, but it could not do enough.

Almost 2,500 years passed before anyone came up with a device that could work better than the abacus. Then, around 1643, a French mathematician named Blaise Pascal made the world's first adding machine. About thirty years later a German named Gottfried von Leiber invented a calculator. Pascal's machine could only add, but the calculator was able to add, subtract, multiply, and divide both quickly and accurately.

After another 200 years a brilliant Englishman, Charles Babbage, conceived an idea for a machine which was far ahead of its time. He called his invention an "analytical engine," because in theory it would be able to work out and analyze any conceivable mathematical problem.

Babbage worked several years on his engine, but while his ideas were sound, he was unable to complete his device because he required other components which had not yet been invented. One of these was the vacuum tube, and the other was the cathode-ray tube.

The first practical computer was made in 1946 by the University of Pennsylvania. This machine contained about 20,000 vacuum tubes and was an engineering marvel. This first true computer was built for the U.S. Government and was installed at the Army Proving Grounds in Aberdeen, Maryland.

Computer science suddenly developed at a rapid rate. Some of these new machines were able to read information from magnetic tape at the rate of more than 70,000 characters a second and perform nearly a billion mathematical operations in a single day.

Modern computers can perform work which would have been impossible only a few years ago, their memory cells storing information until needed and working out problems so complicated that a man with pencil and paper alone might require years to come up with the correct answer.



**The first practical computer was huge, containing some 20,000 vacuum tubes.**
*(U. S. Army)*

# TRANSISTOR

The device demonstrated by three American physicists on June 22, 1948, was no larger than a pea, yet it excited more interest in the scientific world than a nugget of synthetic gold. The product of study and experiment for eight years, the transistor was a radically new device for controlling electrons – a discovery that was destined to replace the vacuum tube in hundreds of appliances and open a new age in electronics.

The transistor met a pressing need. Electronic equipment was becoming more complicated. Scores, or sometimes hundreds or thousands of vacuum tubes had to be crammed into such instruments as high-frequency receivers, telephone amplifiers, and automatic computing machines. Engineers reduced the sizes of tubes, but they continued to give off heat, required much electric power to operate, lasted only a limited time, and often failed at critical moments.

The transistor does the work of most vacuum tubes, never heats up, requires only a small amount of power, lasts indefinitely, and remains almost 100 percent reliable.

The transistor was the result of scientific curiosity. William Shockley, John Bardeen, and Walter Brattain, scientists in the Bell Telephone Laboratories, were interested in the ability of electricity to flow across the surface of a substance called germanium, which was considered practically useless. After many experiments, they created the transistor – which is able to amplify signals as much as 100,000 times.

The first transistors were smaller than vacuum tubes, but they were not small enough. Some modern transistors are so tiny they can be seen clearly only with a microscope!

Today, transistors are used to amplify signals in radios and hearing aids and to open and close circuits in telephone systems, computers, and other instruments. Through the use of transistors, some complicated machines have been made which would have been virtually impossible with vacuum tubes alone.

In recognition of their contribution, Shockley, Bardeen, and Brattain were awarded the Nobel Prize in Physics in 1956.



**The first transistor was developed in 1947 through scientific curiosity.**
***(Bell Telephone Laboratories)***

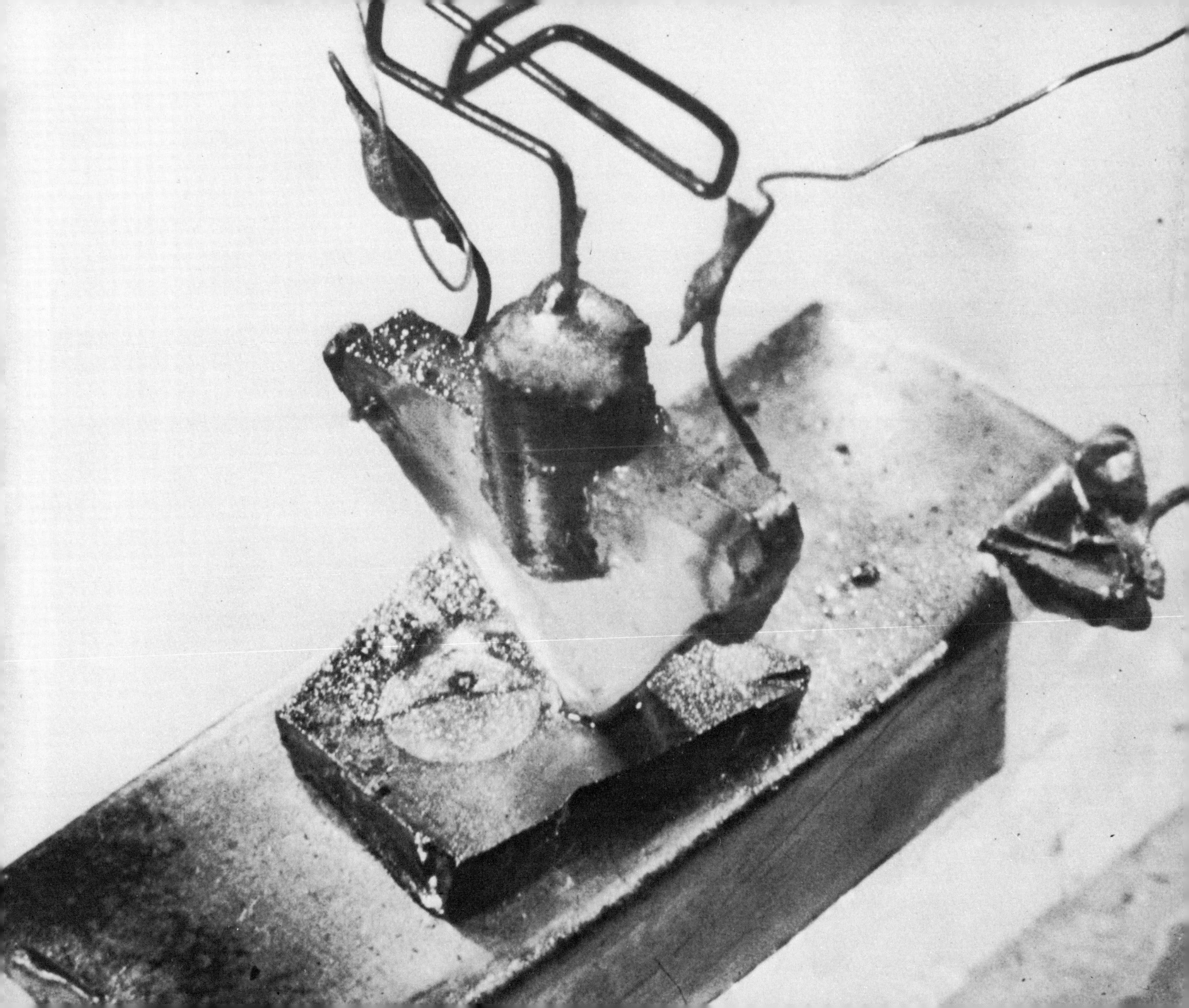

# LASER

The word "laser" is the short form for "light amplification by stimulated emission of radiation." It has turned out to be one of the most amazing devices ever conceived.

The laser has opened a vast new world to science. It can weld metal parts that cannot be joined by any other means; it can even join wires sealed within a glass tube. It can burn a hole through a diamond or a sheet of steel. Theoretically, a thin laser beam could carry 800 million telephone conversations. It can also be used as a surgical tool to perform bloodless operations on the human body in fractions of a second which might require hours by normal means, or which might not be possible at all.

The laser gives off the most powerful light known to man. It can produce temperatures of more than 11,000 degrees Fahrenheit, which is hotter than the sun at its surface. Yet, because of the peculiar properties of laser, this heat can be directed in a very narrow beam.

Unlike normal light, the laser beam does not diffuse. In 1962 a laser beam one foot in diameter was directed at the moon, and it illuminated an area only five feet wide. A beam from a normal light traveling this distance would have spread to a diameter of 25,000 miles. Another advantage of laser light is the fact that it is a pure color and is not composed of a combination of colors as is ordinary light.

With all its advantages, the laser is surprisingly simple. It works on the principle that light is a form of energy. One type of laser has a synthetic ruby coated on both ends by transparent mirrors. A tube coiled around the ruby emits flashes of light which are reflected back and forth between the silvered ends. The atoms of the ruby absorb this energy and become "excited." When the ruby atoms have absorbed their full capacity of energy, they give off a flash of light in a powerful surge.

The first laser was made in 1960 by Theodore Maiman, an American physicist. However, the laser theory was first suggested in 1958 by Charles Townes and Arthur Schawlow, other American scientists.



**The small cube of synthetic ruby at the left is the "heart" of the laser.**
***(Hughes Aircraft Co.)***

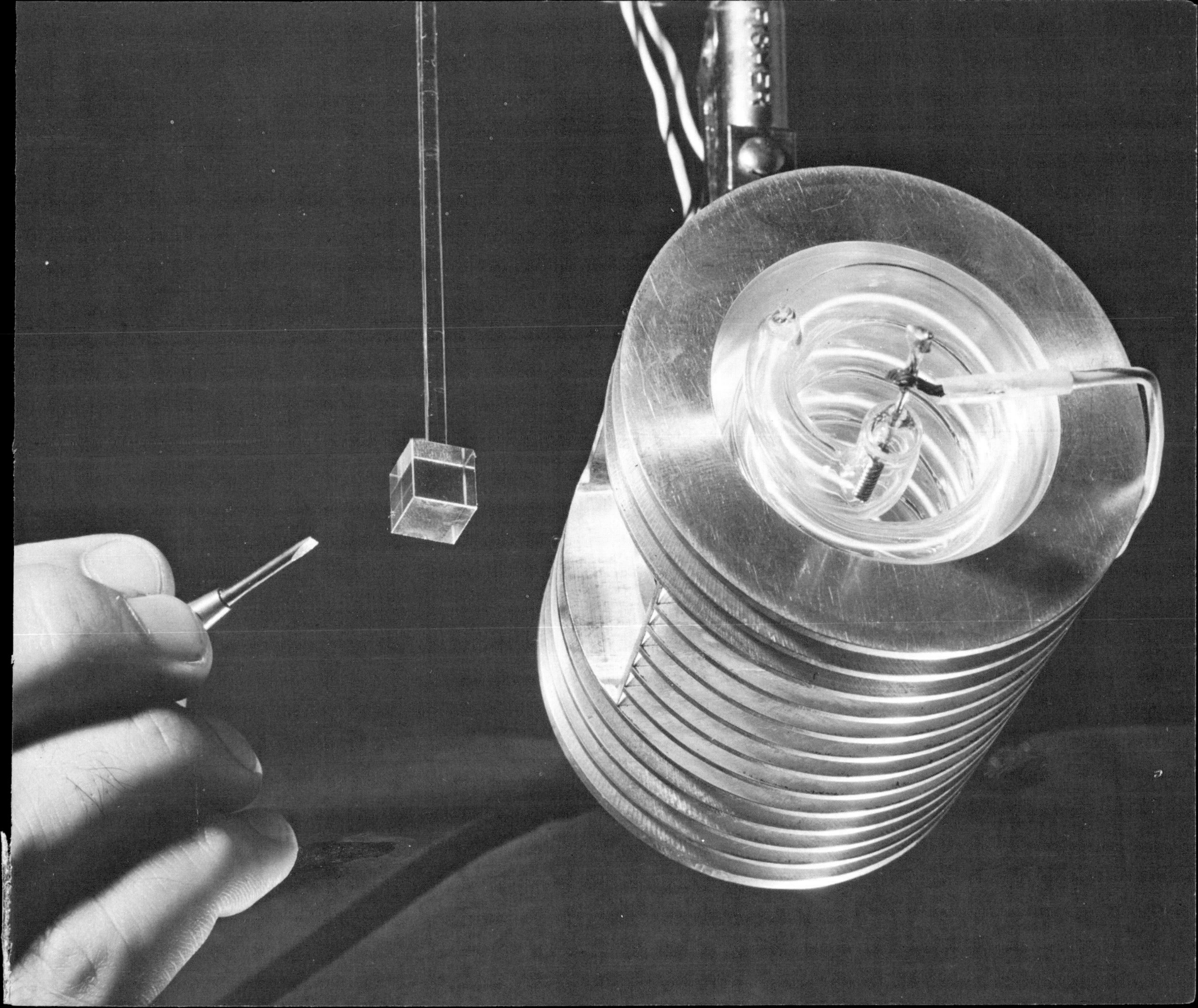

*The Author*

DAVID C. COOKE has traveled extensively and circled the globe three times. He has been a war correspondent (during World War II), a Foreign Service officer for the U.S. government, and a publications adviser to the Vietnamese Ministry of Information. An avid student of man's technological progress, he has devoted most of his writing to magazine articles and books on the engineering sciences. INVENTIONS THAT MADE HISTORY is his seventy-sixth book. Mr. Cooke lives in Valley Stream, New York.